TIMES OF REFRESHING

TIMES OF REFRESHING

Spiritual Rest Stops Along Life's Journey

"...that times of refreshing may come from the Lord..."
Acts 3:19 (NIV)

By

Chinwe L. Ezueh Okpalaoka

Times of Refreshing: Spiritual Rest Stops Along Life's Journey

Published by Chinwe Okpalaoka

ISBN-13: 978-1-7358987-0-4 (Chinwe Okpalaoka)

To honor God, Jesus Christ, and the Holy Spirit, I have capitalized the first letter in the pronouns in reference to Him except where they are used in lowercase in direct quotes. The New Living Translation (NLT) renders YAHWEH as "the LORD" to distinguish it from Adonai, "Lord." This explains the appearance of both names in different forms in this book. I have also capitalized the first letter of "Word" in reference to God's Word, except where it is used in lowercase in direct quotations.

"...that times of refreshing may come from the Lord..."
Acts 3:19 (NIV)

DEDICATION

This book is dedicated to my mother, Cecilia Ezueh, who was the first in our family to encounter and accept Jesus Christ as Lord and Savior. As a result of her obedience, the words of Paul and Silas to the jailer will be fulfilled for her future generations: *"Believe on the Lord Jesus Christ, and you will be saved, you and your household"* (Acts 16:31, NKJV)

ACKNOWLEDGMENTS

I want to thank:

God for the revelation I have received for my own life, through the Holy Spirit, as I study His Word in my private devotions. It is a privilege to share the truths which have brought me much freedom and rest;

My husband, Osita, for your love, encouragement and patience, and for speaking purpose into my work;

My children, Ugonna, Chineze, Dubem and Amara, for the opportunity to extend to you the love I have received from God;

Christy, for "getting" what I am trying to say and helping me express my thoughts better;

My siblings, Ngozi, Nkem and Ik for demonstrating that the bonds of family cannot be easily broken;

My brothers- and sisters-in-love; marriage has made us family;

Friends who support me on many levels, including the YouTube series of the same title as this book

AUTHOR'S NOTE

Have you ever seen one of those time-lapse videos that show, in accelerated motion, what every day occurrences might look like if sped up? Some capture the life cycle of a plant, the development of a child or the construction of a building, all of which typically take time. Do you ever feel that your life is like one of those time-lapse videos, moving at the speed of lightning? Do you sometimes feel like you are on a conveyor belt that never stops as day fades into night and into day again? Well, you are not alone. You are also not alone in wanting to get off the hamster wheel and take a breather. If you want to go the long haul, you need to take breaks to refocus and rejuvenate your mind, body and spirit.

Times of Refreshing: Spiritual Rest Stops Along Life's Journey is a compilation of refreshing reminders to stop and rest in God's Word throughout our day. Each piece, titled as a rest stop or quick stop, invites you to pause, as you would for respite on a long journey. As I complete this book, the world is in a mandatory rest due to the coronavirus pandemic. The streets are eerily empty and all the world institutions we have come to depend on have shut down. We have been forced into a time of deep reflection about the things that really matter.

I pray that as you read this book, that you will begin the practice of enforcing a mandatory rest stop in your life. God is our foundation in a world that can collapse in one day as the last few weeks have demonstrated. Jesus Christ showed us, by example, the importance of making rest stops. He needed these moments of separation to commune with His Father, to get spiritually refreshed to minister to the crowds that made demands on Him. If Jesus needed to stop and commune with

His father, so should we. I hope this book provides an oasis on your life's journey.

REST STOP 1: THE MESSAGE OF THE CROSS– THE POWER OF GOD
(1 CORINTHIANS 1:17-29)

My good friend, Christy, often reminds me that God's Word will speak for itself. She says this when she is proofing a piece I have written, and we are both trying to find the best words to convey the message. We end up yielding to the truth that God will back up His Word with power.

This was the same point Paul was making in his first letter to the Corinthian believers whom he described as having eloquent words and knowledge (1 Corinthians. 1:5). The church at Corinth was beginning to break up into factions and Paul was encouraging them to focus on the main thing: the message of the Cross. Paul reminded them that his assignment from Christ lay in the simple preaching of the Good News of the Gospel, so that the message of the Cross of Christ would not be lost in the multitude of clever words. He wanted them to understand that the power of the Gospel to change hearts and lives was enough without the introduction of human wisdom into the mix. Paul pointed them to a God who, in His wisdom, ensured that the world would never know Him through human wisdom but who would use our foolish preaching to save those who believe (1 Corinthians 1:21).

Many who are called to preach the Gospel do not start off confident. They learn to rely on the Holy Spirit for help. Even Paul, himself, admitted to being timid, anxious and of plain speech, but gave honor to the Holy Spirit who empowered his words so that the hearers would believe in the One who sent him. He declared that faith comes by hearing the Word of God (Romans 10:17).

How does the Holy Spirit help us preach the Good News of the Gospel with power and not with human wisdom? He does it by breathing on the Word of God that we speak and making us able ministers of the Gospel. When we come to faith in Jesus Christ, God's Spirit comes to dwell in our hearts. Then we can hear what He has to say concerning every situation and speak the words that He gives us.

According to Paul, "the natural man does not receive the things of the Spirit of God, for they are foolishness to him; nor can he know them, because they are spiritually discerned" (1 Corinthians 2:14, NKJV). If we want to know the thoughts, plans and deep secrets of God, we must rely on the Holy Spirit in us who discerns the heart of God. Then the Holy Spirit will reveal, to those who love Him and wait for Him, all the wonderful things God has made available to us as we read God's Word.

Before you go: *The message of the Cross does not need to be shared with eloquent words. Just tell the simple story of the redeeming grace of God and He will back up your words with power.*

REST STOP 2: MIND YOUR BUSINESS
(1 CORINTHIANS 3:1-9)

Fall is in the air! I can smell the familiar scents of bonfires, pumpkin spice, and apple cider. I can also hear farming equipment beginning the work of harvesting. This reminds me that there is a process to planting and harvesting. First, the ground is tilled, then the seeds are planted, and finally, the crops are watered and tended until it is harvest time. Every step of the process is equally important. If the ground is not tilled, then the seeds planted in it may die. If the soil is not seeded, then there will be no crops to tend. If the crops are not well-tended, then the harvest will be poor.

Paul used the agricultural metaphor when he admonished the Corinthian church for the quarrels and jealousies that were threatening to divide them. Some were claiming allegiance to Paul and others to Apollos, and Paul warned that this behavior was an indication that they were still being controlled by their flesh and not by the Holy Spirit. He had to remind them that he and Apollos were just God's servants through whom God brought the Good News of the Gospel. The field (the Corinthians) belonged to God and they, Paul and Apollos, were mere workers in God's field. Paul explained, "each of us did the work the Lord gave us" (1 Corinthians 3:5b, NLT).

What was the work of these servants of God? Paul was the planter of the seed of the Gospel and Apollos was the one who came behind to water the seed. God brought the harvest because only He can make the seeds grow. Paul was simply asking the Corinthians to mind their business. Instead of trying to determine who had the most important role in God's kingdom-building, Paul was asking the Corinthians to focus on following the God who brings the increase.

Whether you sow or water, the purpose of our assignments as believers is the same, and God will reward you according to the work you have done (1 Corinthians 3:8; Revelation 22:12). It is very easy to get caught up in the mundane tasks of daily living and lose focus of your calling in Christ. When you are jealous of the work other people are doing to help advance God's kingdom, you lose sight of the task God has committed to you.

Kingdom building is not like competitive sports with everyone striving to be the champion. There are no winners in kingdom-building. Instead, the work calls for every member of the body of Christ to identify the role they have been assigned and do it "as though you were working for the Lord rather than for people" (Colossians 3:23, NLT). If you are not sure of your calling, ask God to show you and He will make it clear. He is the same God who says, "this is the way; walk in it" (Isaiah 30:21, NIV). When He has shown you what He requires of you, put your hand to the plow and don't look back (Luke 9:62).

Before you go: *What do you think you have been called to do as a member of God's family? Are you doing it? If not, what is stopping you?*

REST STOP 3: SCUM OF THE EARTH?
(MATTHEW 9:9-13)

When Jesus called Matthew to become His disciple, He knew Matthew was a tax collector, one of the despised professions of that time. But He did not say, "Matthew, you filthy tax-collector, repent, follow me and be my disciple!" He simply said, "Follow me and be my disciple!" And Matthew got up and followed Jesus. On his part, Matthew did not question what Jesus wanted with a scum like himself. He may not have thought of himself as scum in that moment; after all, he dared to invite Jesus, along with his other tax collector friends, into his home.

When the Pharisees saw this interaction, they were not pleased. They wondered why the Teacher was eating with a man they considered to be scum. You would think that they would have learned from experience the type of people Jesus was drawn to. Jesus responded to them, and I paraphrase, "I came for the scum of the earth, the sick, and the rejects" (Matthew 9:12). The Pharisees thought they were righteous keepers and perfecters of the law, but Jesus did not come for those who "think" they are righteous. He came for those who "know" they are sinners.

A similar scenario played out again when Jesus confronted another group of Pharisees "who had great confidence in their righteousness and scorned everyone else" (Luke 18:9, NLT). This time, Jesus used a parable to compare a Pharisee who was blind to his sins and did not think he needed to repent and a tax collector who was ashamed of his sins and filled with sorrowful repentance. In the end, it was the tax collector whose sins were forgiven.

There is a difference between thinking you are righteous and knowing you are a sinner. Jesus will take the latter any day because He came for sinners. It is easy for pride and self-righteousness to subtly creep into our consciousness. It can happen when we compare ourselves to others and think that we are better than them or when we allow a critical spirit to snuff out the opportunity to be merciful to others.

Jesus used the stories of the Pharisees and tax collectors to teach us not to think too highly of ourselves because "those who exalt themselves will be humbled, and those who humble themselves will be exalted" (Luke 18:14, NLT). I don't know about you, but the thought of being brought down from a pedestal sounds uncomfortable to me. When He declared that He wants us to show mercy, not offer sacrifices (Hosea 6:6), Jesus was teaching us about His value for a repentant heart that desperately needs the Savior and not a righteous, self-sufficient heart.

Before you go: It is very easy to slip into self-righteousness, especially when we compare ourselves to those who we consider to be worse than we are. These are the very ones Jesus came to save.

QUICK STOP: WHAT FOUNTAIN ARE YOU DRINKING FROM?

Jeremiah asks: "Has anyone ever heard of anything as strange as this? Has any nation ever traded its gods for new ones, even though they are not gods at all? Yet my people have exchanged their glorious God for worthless idols! ... they have abandoned me – the fountain of living water. And they have dug for themselves cracked cisterns that can hold no water at all" (Jeremiah 2:10-13, NLT). Yes, we often trade our God for idols, for things that occupy the preeminent place in our hearts meant for Him alone. We abandon Him again and again, drinking from foul, smelly waters instead of from the fountain of living waters. Centuries later, Jesus promised fresh, life-giving living water to the woman at the well (John 4:10). He also proclaimed, "I am the way, the truth, and the life" (John 14:6, NLT). We still need the living water today. It gives life and nourishment to our thirsty souls. It satisfies like nothing else will. Why do we work hard at digging our own cracked, unproductive wells to find our own water, when God has done all the work for us? Jesus said: "Whoever believes in me, as

Scripture has said, rivers of living water will flow from within them" (John 7:38, NIV). We need not labor for that which does not satisfy.

The work has already been done on our behalf. Just drink to your satisfaction, to the fullest, till it overflows!

REST STOP 4: ALWAYS BEGIN WITH AN ALTAR
(EZRA 1:1-7; 3:1-6)

God remembers His promises and keeps them. He promised the children of Israel that, in the fullness of time, when seventy years of exile in Babylon were over, He would bring them back to their homeland. He fulfilled His promise through the most unlikely person, the Babylonian King Cyrus, who had everything to lose by setting the Israelites free. God stirred Cyrus' heart to return the articles which his father, Nebuchadnezzar, had seized from the temple in Jerusalem when he conquered the Israelites. Cyrus also stirred the hearts of the Babylonians to give the returnees valuable gifts to help in their resettlement.

The Israelites were very thankful to God for keeping His promise and their first task, once they were settled in Jerusalem, was to build an altar to God where they worshipped Him day and night according to the requirements of the Law. We learn that they did all this even before they laid the foundation of the Temple. They knew that the altar was crucial to the task of rebuilding.

They could have waited until the foundation was laid, or the temple completed, before building an altar, but the returnees knew that beginning with worship was necessary for the work ahead. They knew that if they accorded God His rightful and preeminent place in their plans, then His Presence would be with them as they rebuilt.

How many times have you postponed spending time in prayer and worship until after all the chores are completed? You always think you'll concentrate better if you finish other things first, but it never works that way. The altar is still important today when you are presented with opportunities for fresh starts. Your fresh start could be a new day, a new home, a new church or a new job. Start where you are and don't wait for all your prayers to be answered and for everything to fall into place before you build an altar. Worship enthrones God in all His power, might and authority and causes whatever situations we may face to pale in comparison to who He is.

Before you go: *Today, your altar does not need to be a physical one. It is any place you set aside to worship God with all your heart, mind and strength.*

REST STOP 5: THE FUTILITY OF LOOKING BACK
(EZRA 3:7-12)

The altar had been built and it was now time to work on the temple's foundation. Because the returnees were bound by a unified purpose, everyone played a part in the work. We learn that once they had laid the foundation of the temple, they paused again for a praise break. They sang to the Lord, declaring His goodness and His faithfulness which endures forever (Ezra 3:11).

But there was a group of people who did not join the praise break. These were the older priests and Levites who had seen the first temple in all its glory. They looked back with regret at the past, the old temple and the old ways, and compared these to the new work God was doing. In so doing, they missed that God was doing a new thing.

It is important to note that those older priests and Levites were not comparing two similar things. They were comparing the first temple in its completed and glorious state to the foundation of the new temple. If they had waited patiently to see the new temple in its completed state, they might have understood God's plan. Those who understood the times rejoiced at the new thing. They trusted in the God who promised, "Behold, I will do a new thing; Now it shall spring forth; Shall you not know it? I will even make a road in the wilderness, And rivers in the desert" (Isaiah 43:19, NKJV).

At some time or another, we have all come to a crossroads where we either had to choose to go forward and embrace the future God has planned for us or look back and long for the way things used to be. I have discovered that I prefer a future with God in it than a past that is over. New seasons always bring new promises better than anything we can imagine. Any time you face a new beginning, a fresh start, don't be preoccupied with longing for the things that are over and done with. Instead, trust God to reveal His complete plans for your life. And when He does, let go of the old and embrace the new!

Before you go: *If you drive looking in the rearview mirror, you will hit the car in front of you. Likewise, if you keep looking back at the past, you will miss out on the better things God has ahead of you.*

QUICK STOP: AH! WHAT RELIEF!

What joy and peace to know that my efforts could not achieve for me what Christ did over 2,000 years ago at Golgotha! There have been many times I have tried to focus on perfecting my own efforts, but all I have gotten in return, every time, have been weary, drooping shoulders, weak from carrying burdens that were not meant for me to carry. Hasn't He invited me to cast my cares, worries and anxieties on Him because He cares for me (1 Peter 5:7)? Haven't I read, many times, that I should come to Him, when I am weary and heavy-burdened, and He will give me rest, for His yoke is easy and His burden is light (Matthew 11:28-30)? Why have I, then, been insistent on being my own burden-bearer? Is it because I think I am a better manager of my own affairs? Still, He has waited patiently for me to literally fall on my face, until I take my hands off and just rest. One day, over 2,000 years ago, He announced, "It is finished!" The work is done! Christ finished the work that day so that you and I will cease striving. Rest, brothers and sisters, rest!

REST STOP 6: LET ME PRAY ABOUT IT
(2 CHRONICLES 18:1-7)

It's true what they say about finding the answers to life's questions in the Bible and I was recently reminded of the problem with forming wrong alliances and acting on your own wisdom and judgment. Jehoshaphat king of Judah, and Ahab King of Israel were in-laws. Jehoshaphat's son was married to Ahab's daughter. One day, while Ahab was entertaining his in-law, he asked Jehoshaphat to ally with him in a war to recover a land and people that had been taken from him. There was nothing wrong with this request. After all they were family and family should do what they can to support one another, right? Jehoshaphat's response was, "of course...but first, let's find out what the LORD says" (2 Chronicles 18:4, NLT).

When I read his simple response, I was impressed and convicted at once. I am sure you know how difficult it can be to say "No" to people, especially the ones you love. I struggle, sometimes, with feeling that I am disappointing them when I don't respond in the manner they expect. Ahab summoned his own prophets, the ones he paid to prophesy *only* the things he wanted to hear, and they advised him to proceed to war. But Jehoshaphat wanted to hear from a prophet of God, one who would not be afraid to speak the truth.

Micaiah was such a prophet and he warned both Kings not to go to war because King Ahab would lose his life. The rest is history. King Ahab disobeyed, went to the war in disguise, and asked Jehoshaphat to fight in his own kingly robes so he would become the target of the enemy's army. True to Micaiah's prophesy, Ahab died in the war (despite his plot to have Jehoshaphat killed in his place). We don't know why Jehoshaphat ignored Micaiah's prophesy and formed an alliance with Ahab, but he must have learned in that battle that there is a consequence to disobeying Godly counsel. The same lesson is very relevant to us today. It is okay to say, "Let me pray about it!" We can seek God's counsel in the seemingly small as well as in the serious matters of life. And the good news is that we do not need to consult a prophet. God speaks directly to our hearts if we only ask.

After the war was over, Jehoshaphat heard from another prophet, Jehu, the folly of helping the wicked and loving those who hate the Lord (2 Chronicles 19:2). Jehu confirmed what I believe was the reason Jehoshaphat's life was spared. Unlike many kings before him, he had removed the idols in the land and committed himself to seeking God. Jehoshaphat spent the rest of his reign encouraging the people to return to the Lord, the God of their ancestors- a lesson he had learned very well.

Today, you, too, will benefit from seeking Godly counsel in all matters. Doing so will give you the clarity you need to make life decisions.

Before you go: *It is better to spend a few minutes seeking Godly counsel than a lifetime facing the consequences of doing things your own way.*

REST STOP 7: ROOF-RAISING FRIENDS
(MARK 2:1-12)

Have you ever seen one or more of those sentimental online articles about the different types of friends everyone needs? I have always loved the one about the friends who know when to come in and carry you out to save you from making a fool of yourself. I don't know about you, but I need friends like that. The paralytic man in Mark 2 also needed radical friends—the ones who will stage an intervention to either save your life or save you from yourself.

The news had spread that Jesus was in town and a large crowd thronged around him, but the paralytic's four friends did not let that deter them from accomplishing their mission. When they realized that they might be carrying their friend back home in his current condition, they became desperate. They had to find another way to get their friend to Him about whom Luke proclaimed, "And the Lord's healing power was strongly with Jesus" (Luke 5: 17, NLT).

While Luke's account says that the friends took off some tiles from the roof, Mark's version describes how they dug a hole through the roof above Jesus' head. This allowed the men to lower their friend right into Jesus' Presence. Then, "seeing their faith, Jesus said to the paralyzed man, 'My child, your sins are forgiven'" (Mark 2:5, NLT).

We will all come to a time in our lives when we cannot go it alone and those desperate times will demand desperate measures. We don't know how long the paralytic had longed to get to Jesus. We also don't know what conversations transpired between him and his friends that day. But what is apparent is that he had friends who did not give up on him. Where the strength of their friend failed him, they became his strength. Jesus noticed what the four men had done and was moved to act on the faith they had displayed on behalf of their friend.

This is the point where you may be tempted to start taking mental stock of your friendships: "Do I have friends who would go the extra mile for me? Do I have friends who will be my voice when I can't speak?" But before you start assessing what type of friends you have, how about you begin by asking, "Am I a roof-raising kind of friend?" We should aspire to be the kind of friends we want—friends who will contend on our behalf for our breakthrough.

Before you go: *Be the kind of friend that you will love to have.*

REST STOP 8: HOW HEALTHY ARE YOUR EYES?
(MATTHEW 6:22-23)

A popular proverb says that the eyes are a window to the soul—meaning that the eyes reflect the goings-on in our souls. Jesus, too, alluded to the power of the human eyes to not only reflect but determine the state of one's health. He likened the eye to a lamp: "Your eye is like a lamp that provides light for your body. When your eye is healthy, your whole body is filled with light. But when your eye is unhealthy, your whole body is filled with darkness. And if the light you think you have is actually darkness, how deep that darkness is" (Matthew 6:22-23, NLT).

Jesus distinguished between a healthy eye and an unhealthy eye. A healthy eye is not paranoid. It is not quick to judge what it sees and is always ready to give the benefit of doubt. A healthy eye knows that there is usually more to a situation than meets the eye (pun intended). When our eyes are healthy, we are gracious and merciful towards others. We are not easily offended. An unhealthy eye is suspicious of everything. It is distrustful and quick to rush to judgment, to take everything at face value or imagine things that aren't real. An unhealthy eye is not compassionate and does not consider that there could be more to a story. An unhealthy eye will write you off in a second.

So how healthy are your eyes? How well do you see and how do you react to what you see? Are you quick to take offense or are you quick to extend grace? It may be a glance, a certain tone of voice, a careless word or the inflection on a certain word and offense can quickly take root. Soon relationships break down, hurtful words are traded, and months roll into years without a resolution. Many times, the disintegration of a relationship is the result of an erroneous perception. For example, you unexpectedly run into a friend. Your face lights up with recognition and you approach her with a smile, ready to share pleasantries about your lives. As you approach her, she greets you casually and walks past you. What is your first reaction? Are you immediately offended and begin to wonder why she has practically ignored you? Are you reminded of a similar incident in the past when she behaved the same way? Do you decide that you have had enough and will mind your business next time? If these are some of the thoughts that might pass through your mind, Jesus says your eye is unhealthy and your whole body is filled with darkness.

Let us replay that scene again. If your eye is healthy, then your perception of your friend's actions will be different because "your whole body is filled with light." You will not be quick to judge her actions as a dismissal of you. You will find her behavior odd, but you will also be concerned about her. You will wonder if she is having a difficult day, week, month. You will wonder what matters are weighing heavily on her mind. You may even consider whether you unintentionally offended her the last time you were together. And because your eye is healthy, you will look for an opportunity to connect, to clarify, to seek peace and to heal.

In the Beatitudes, Jesus taught about the blessings that accompany peacemakers and those who extend mercy to others. He said that if you are merciful, you will obtain mercy when you need it. If you are a peacemaker, you will be called the son or daughter of God because He is your Father, Jehovah Shalom, the God of Peace Himself (Matthew 5:9). You can only extend mercy and seek peace if you perceive your world through healthy eyes because healthy eyes mean a body (spirit, soul and body) that is healthy and filled with light. Then you will be able to be the light that shines in a dark world, a city set on a hill that cannot be hidden (Matthew 5:14).

Therefore, let your light so shine before men and women so that they may see your good works which stem from a light-filled body (Matthew 5:16). As a result, they will give all the glory to your Father in heaven.

Before you go: *How healthy are your spiritual eyes? Ask God to fill you with His light so that you can see as He does.*

QUICK STOP: THE GOLDEN RULE

"Do to others as you would like them to do to you" (Luke 6:31, NLT). How do you want to be treated? That is a good place to start. I know I want mercy and grace when I hurt others. I want to be given second and third chances. I want to be forgiven and not expected to be forever indebted to the people I hurt. If I want all these things, then I must be willing to respond similarly to others. Jesus reminded His disciples that everything they had received from Him was free and that they were to be equally generous to others. We are not to crave mercy from others and then be selfish in extending the same.

REST STOP 9: GET UP! PICK UP YOUR MAT AND WALK!
(JOHN 5:1-9)

Ashes symbolize a place of death and mourning. There is no life there. In some cultures, mourners sit among the ashes until their time of mourning is over. Are you an ash-dweller? Have you comfortably made your home among the ashes of your dashed dreams? Are you so caught up in what might have been that your present life is passing you by? Do you live in regret of a past that you cannot change? Then it is time to "Get up! Pick up your mat and walk" (John 5:8, NIV)!

This was the command that Jesus gave to the man who had been lying beside the pool of Bethesda for thirty-eight years. He does not have a name, but he could easily be any one of us. He deserved to feel sorry for himself and have Jesus feel sorry for him. After all, nothing could have been worse than watching others jump into the healing waters of the pool, year after year, while the man was stuck in his misery and could not see a way out.

As soon as Jesus encountered him, all He asked the man was, "Would you like to get well" (John 5:6, NLT)? Why did Jesus ask a sick man if he wanted to get well? Wasn't that an obvious question? After all, we are told that Jesus "saw him and knew he had been ill for a long time..." (John 5:6, NLT). The man's response explains Jesus' question very clearly. He responded with the excuses many of us use in our own lives: "I can't! Poor me! I am all alone! Nobody loves me! Nobody wants to help me! Others cheat me and take advantage of my circumstances. I will never get well! My situation is going to last forever!" But Jesus simply responded, "Get up! Pick up your mat and walk." Jesus was a compassionate man because he had extended compassion to others in different circumstances, but

He knew that in this instance, time was of the essence. This man had to be delivered from his thirty-eight-year pity party. Furthermore, his healing had to be tied to his obedience. We know that he got up, picked up his mat and walked.

Today, God is still asking, "Would you like to get well"? You, too, can rise out of the ashes you have dwelled in for so long. For you, it may not have been thirty-eight years, but it has been long enough. God is waiting for you to respond in obedience. He wants you to desperately want to be made whole. He wants to give you beauty in exchange for the ashes of your broken dreams; to give you the oil of joy instead of the mourning in your heart from broken dreams; to give you a garment of praise in place of the garments of mourning you are wearing (Isaiah 61:3).

So do not despise the day of small beginnings (Zechariah 4:10). You can begin today. "Today, if you hear His voice, do not harden your heart..." (Hebrews 3:15, NIV). You do not want to wake up thirty-eight years from now and realize that you forgot to live. Selah!

Before you go: *Today, God is asking you, "Do you want to get well?" This is another chance to get up and walk by faith in God's purpose for your life. It is not too late!*

REST STOP 10: ABOVE ALL
(LUKE 22:32; 1 PETER 4:8)

Simon Peter was the spontaneous disciple. He was the one who jumped into the water at Jesus' bidding to come to Him, the one who cut off the ear of the high priest's slave who was among the Roman contingent which came to arrest Jesus, and the one who swore that he would be loyal to Jesus even unto death. He did not know what Jesus already knew: that Peter's love for Jesus was clothed in human frailty and that he would soon deny ever being with Jesus. That was why Jesus prayed for Peter's faith not to fail in the hours leading up to Jesus' death.

Peter eventually denied his association with Jesus and was deeply repentant when he realized what he had done. One Gospel account describes the look that Jesus gave Peter the third time he denied knowing Jesus. After Jesus' crucifixion, the disciples dispersed and went back to their fishing business. They went back to what was familiar.

After His resurrection, Jesus appeared to His disciples three times, but it wasn't until His third appearance that we get some insight into Peter's redemption. Jesus found the disciples after a night of an unsuccessful fishing expedition. He called out to them from the shore and directed them to the best fishing spot. When Peter realized it was Jesus on the shore, he forgot the pain, hurt and bitterness that accompanied his betrayal of Jesus. Once again, he became the spontaneous Peter Jesus knew. He jumped into the water and headed to the shore. He did not shrink back in shame or fear. It was almost as if Peter connected this encounter by the sea with the very first time he responded to the call to follow Jesus. Jesus' perfect love had cast out any fear Peter felt prior to this encounter. Imagine the relief and freedom that Peter must have felt in the warm embrace of the Savior's love.

As they all broke bread together on the shore, Peter got the wonderful opportunity to experience Jesus' love and forgiveness and Jesus renewed His covenant with Peter again, instructing him, "Follow me!" No wonder Peter was able to write later, "Above all, love each other deeply, because love covers a multitude of sins" (1 Peter 4:8, NIV). He had experienced the deep love of the Master, which covered his betrayal of Jesus. Later, he would teach others to do the same. This was what Jesus prophesied about Peter in the hours leading up to His crucifixion: "So when you have repented and turned to me again, strengthen your brothers" (Luke 22:32, NLT).

Today, if you are afraid that your sins have separated you from God, He is inviting you: "Follow me!" There is nothing that His perfect love will not forgive if you turn to Him. And when you have received this love, extend it towards others. Freely you have received; freely give (Matthew 10:8, NIV)!

Before you go: *You will never be too far gone for God to reach you with His love. When you have received God's love, remember to extend the same to others.*

REST STOP 11: THE GOD WHO IS NEAR
(PSALM 135:15-17)

It is futile to craft an idol with your own hands and then worship it as god (Isaiah 46:6-7). The book of Psalms talks about the futility of worshipping man-made gods. The Psalmist, David, compared these inanimate objects, crafted by their creators, with the God of Israel who demonstrated great power and might when He brought the children of Israel out of captivity in Egypt. He declared: "I know the greatness of the LORD—that our Lord is greater than any other god" (Psalm 135:5, NLT).

In another Psalm, David extolled the God who is not distant from human reach; the God who stoops down to connect with His creation. He inquired, "Who can be compared with the LORD our God, who is enthroned on high? He stoops to look down on heaven and earth" (Psalm 113:5-6, NLT). In all His majesty, God still concerns Himself with humanity. That is why David declared his love for the Lord who bends down to listen and hears his prayer for mercy. No wonder he swore an oath to pray to this God for as long as he had breath in him.

I am encouraged by the image of a God who stoops down, who bends down to listen, to connect with His creation. He is approachable and desires intimate fellowship with us. Speaking of Israel's rebellion after He had delivered them from Egypt, God said, "I lifted the yoke from [Israel's] neck, and I myself stooped to feed him" (Hosea 11:4, NLT). Even when we rebel and choose to go our own way, God does not abandon us. His eyes still roam to and fro the earth seeking to show Himself strong on behalf of those whose hearts are committed to Him (2 Chronicles 16:9). On the morning after a particularly challenging day, the reminder that God is not far away from me reassures me. I recall where He also spoke about Himself: "Before they call, I will answer; while they are still speaking, I will hear" (Isaiah 65:24, NIV). This sounds, to me, like a God who is always near.

Before you go*: Take God at His Word that He is always by your side, and then be strengthened by that truth.*

REST STOP 12: ARE YOU LEAKING?
(MATTHEW 12:33-37)

"For my people have done two evil things: They have abandoned me—the fountain of living water. And they have dug for themselves cracked cisterns that can hold no water at all" (Jeremiah 2:13, NLT)! God was speaking metaphorically about His people's abandonment of Him for the created gods of the nations around them. Earlier in this book, I talked about this verse from Jeremiah, but I am revisiting it from another perspective. My focus, then, was on what fountains we drink from as believers. This time, I will be looking at how the contents of our hearts, what we consume spiritually, determine what comes out of us.

Speaking to His people through the prophet Jeremiah, God admonished them concerning two matters: first, He was no longer their primary focus; they were no longer seeking Him for the living water that quenches all human longings. Secondly, they had dug their own cisterns. They had become a rebellious people, and seeking to be self-sufficient, they forgot about El-Shaddai, the All-Sufficient God. They found the proliferation of other gods more attractive because these gods made no demands of them. The only problem was that their cisterns were leaking.

According to the Merriam-Webster dictionary, a cistern is an artificial reservoir used for storing liquids like rainwater. In other words, a cistern is a man-made, water collection and storage system. It is a typology of self-sufficiency, of man trying to harness nature for his benefit. Cisterns can develop leaks and need to be carefully monitored and maintained. Like cisterns we, too, are reservoirs. Our hearts are storage systems, serving as repositories for attributes such as rebellion, pride, bitterness, fear, unforgiveness, envy and selfishness. Like cisterns, our hearts can also crack and leak out; therefore, it is important to stop occasionally and take stock of what we have stored up in our hearts. For example, what thoughts do you think? What do these look like when you leak?

As Scripture reminds us, as a man thinks in his heart, so is he (Proverbs 23:7). Elsewhere we read that "a good man brings good things out of the good stored up in him, and an evil man brings evil things out of the evil stored up in him" (Matthew 12:35, NIV). Like the children of Israel, we, too, rebel when we choose to go our own way and rely on our strength and limited wisdom. It is only a matter of time before a crack develops to remind us of the limitations of trusting in our ability to run our lives. Soon, rebellion, pride, bitterness, fear, unforgiveness, envy and selfishness start to leak out of the abundance of our hearts. But it does not have to be that way.

The God who did not give up on Israel will not give up on us. He asks us to return to Him because His mercy and His anger do not last forever. What fountain are you drinking from? Or are you drawing from your own cracked cistern? Check for leaks, and you may very well discover from what water supply you have been drinking.

Before you go: *Feed only on the things that nourish your spirit. Then out of the reservoir of your heart will flow life and Godliness.*

QUICK STOP: I AM A WITNESS

God loves you! Sounds so cliché, but it is so real, so pure and so true. This is a time-tested truth. I have known His love; I have experienced it. I am honored because He loves me (Isaiah 43:4). There is no other like Him—I am a witness. To demonstrate His amazing love, He chose us to know Him, to believe in Him and to understand that He is God and there is no one that can compare (Isaiah 43:10). Yes, I am a witness that from eternity to eternity, indeed from everlasting to everlasting, He is God. NO ONE can snatch you from His hands, no NOTHING! No one can undo what God has done and planned for your life. So, today, Holy Spirit is reminding us to forget the former things, the things that are past, over, done with and embrace with expectancy the new thing God is doing. Even now He has already begun the good thing and I see it, I sense it. He WILL make a pathway in the wilderness and rivers in the dry places (Isaiah 43:19).

REST STOP 13: WHAT DO YOU WANT ME TO DO FOR YOU?
(MARK 10:46-52)

I know what it is like to be desperate, to come to my wit's end, and to the end of my understanding of everything I think I know. I know what it is to become fully aware of my human limitations and need for divine intervention. This is the position in which Bartimaeus found himself the day Jesus passed by. He was doubly disadvantaged; he was a blind beggar who was very aware of not only his disadvantages, but of his surroundings. He had heard about Jesus and believed everything he had heard about him. He had heard Jesus' voice commanding the sick to be whole, blinded eyes to open and dead situations to come alive. He had heard the shouts of amazement, joy and excitement that accompanied these miracles. He had probably heard Jesus' critics question his integrity as well as the whispers of the ones who wanted Jesus dead.

So, when he heard Jesus was nearby, he raised his voice in desperation so he could be heard above the crowd that thronged around him: "Jesus, Son of David, have mercy on me" (Mark 10:47, NLT)! The more the crowd tried to silence him, the louder Bartimaeus shouted in desperation. I know that cry, too. I have cried it aloud and I have whispered it in my heart. When you have come to the end of your rope and to the end of human effort, you become desperate for Him who said, "My grace is sufficient for you, for my power is made perfect in weakness" (2 Corinthians 12:9, NIV). When everything you know intellectually fails you, you declare as King Jehoshaphat did when his people were faced with vast armies beyond their own might: "We do not know what to do, but our eyes are on you" (2 Chronicles 20:12, NIV). Desperation attracts God's attention.

It signals an acknowledgment of His mighty power. Bartimaeus' cry caused Jesus to stop in His tracks and request that Bartimaeus be brought to Him. "What do you want me to do for you?" Jesus asked him. Very simply and without hesitation Bartimaeus responded, "Rabbi, I want to see" (Mark 10:51, NIV). When, like Bartimaeus, I cry out to Jesus I, too, want to see. I want to see the situation I am in through His vantage point because leaning on my own understanding distorts my view. All He asks is that I trust Him and place my faith in He who is greater than me.

Bartimaeus' faith stopped Jesus in his tracks and Jesus healed him. Without faith it is impossible to please God. Anyone who comes to God must believe that He exists and that He rewards those who diligently and desperately seek Him (Hebrews 11:6). What do you want Him to do for you, today? Perhaps you can start with acknowledging your limitations and simply crying out to Him: "I want to see!" He will cause you to see as He sees, and you will discover that His perspective wins every time.

Before you go: *Seeking and receiving God's perspective on our circumstances brings clarity. Do you want to see as God sees? Simply ask Him who gives freely.*

REST STOP 14: LOOK UP!
(ISAIAH 40:25-31)

Reading from the daily devotion one morning, I obeyed God's command through the prophet Isaiah to lift my eyes and look to the heavens (Isaiah 40:26). I lifted my eyes and looked through the tall windows of my living room. As I did, I became engrossed in the clear skies and the clouds that moved slowly along. Then it occurred to me that the clouds I saw one minute before had moved on and were no longer there. I enjoyed this vantage point and welcomed the peace that overcame me as I enjoyed the view. "I should do this more often," I thought to myself.

God asked in Isaiah 40, "To whom will you compare me? Or who is my equal? Lift up your eyes and look to the heavens: Who created all these" (v. 25-26a, NIV)? As I continued to look upwards, I realized how much time I spend looking down and around me. The vast skies reminded me of how small I am and how insignificant today's burdens will be tomorrow—just like the clouds that appear one minute and slowly drift away the next.

Then my upward gaze shifted to "He who brings out the starry host one by one and calls forth each of them by name. Because of his great power and mighty strength, not one of them is missing" (v. 26b, NIV). Think about this. If He laid out the skies like canopies and hung the stars, sun and moon in their rightful places, "Why do you complain, [insert your name here]? Why do you say, [insert your name here], "my way is hidden from the Lord; my cause is disregarded by my God"? Do you not know? Have you not heard? The Lord is the everlasting God, the Creator of the ends of the earth. He will not grow tired or weary, and his understanding no one can fathom" (v. 27-28, NIV).

There are moments when I grow weary of waiting for a promise. I know you do, too. The circumstances around you do not reflect that for which you are holding on in faith. But Isaiah is saying, "hold on and do not faint." God's Word gives us fresh perspective today and every day thereafter. Your hopelessness or weariness do not surprise Him. That is why He has made provision way ahead of your need: "He gives strength to the weary and increases the power of the weak. Even youths grow tired and weary, and young men stumble and fall; but those who hope in the Lord will renew their strength. They will soar on wings like eagles; they will run and not grow weary; they will walk and not be faint" (v. 29-31, NIV). So, lift your eyes! Look to the heavens and be strengthened!

Before you go*: When life's challenges come, remember to look up and not around you.*

REST STOP 15: MAKE ROOM FOR THE PROPHET– HOSTING THE PRESENCE OF GOD
(2 KINGS 4:8-36)

She had no agenda. She had no predetermined expectations of the prophet. The wealthy woman from Shunem had everything she needed, but she recognized what Elisha carried: the Presence of God. So, she invited him into her home and, soon, made a permanent place for him to stay whenever he was in town. She made room for the Presence of God (2 Kings 4:9-10).

Her generosity touched Elisha, and he wanted to return the favor, but the woman refused. The Presence of God was more than enough for her. She knew that nothing the prophet could give her would compare to the blessing of God's Presence. For as the Psalmist declared, "In [His] Presence is fullness of joy; In [His] right hand there are pleasures forever" (Psalm 16:11, NASB).

Elisha persisted in his desire to reward the woman, so when he learned that she longed for a son, he prophesied that she would have one by the same time next year. Elisha's prophecy came to pass. It is no surprise, then, that years later, when the woman's son fell sick and died, she laid him in the room she had prepared for the prophet and shut the door. Her immediate declaration of faith was, "It is well!" She set out to look for the prophet, believing once again that he carried within him what she needed. She did not waver in her faith but stood firm in her pursuit so that when Elisha offered to send his servant in his place to raise the boy, the woman refused, saying, "As surely as the LORD lives and you yourself live, I won't go home unless you go with me" (2 Kings 4:30, NLT). Elisha relented, followed her home, and raised the boy.

How do you host the Presence of God? First, you need to be able to recognize Him. The woman from Shunem recognized that Elisha was a holy man of God and she understood what he carried within him. If you hang around carriers of God's Presence, you will become familiar with Him, too. Secondly, you need to make room in your life, home, and heart for Him. This includes setting apart space and time to commune with God. Like all relationships, time spent together leads to greater intimacy. Finally, making space for the Presence means getting rid of junk from your life, home and heart. God's Presence cannot jostle for space with clutter.

The Shunammite woman made room for God's Presence, and for her kindness towards the prophet, she received the miracle of life—twice.

Before you go: *Seek God's presence and in it will be everything that you will ever need.*

REST STOP 16: A LIFE RESTORED
(MARK 5:22-42)

My name is Jairus, and my daughter is sick. I have just heard about the man whom Jesus delivered from a legion of demons. That is huge, I think. If He can do that for a man who has been terrorizing the town, then he can heal my twelve-year-old daughter. I am an important man, a ruler of the synagogue, but that means nothing right now because I am desperate – desperate enough to fall at Jesus' feet and plead for my daughter's life. And, just like that, Jesus agrees to come to my home.

But how can I keep the crowd away from Him? Everybody seems to want something. And this woman who is crouching at his feet? Why is she grabbing a hold of the hem of Jesus' garment? Doesn't she see He is in a hurry? My daughter lies at the point of death. Now Jesus is stopping to talk to her. Does He not understand the urgency of my need? Does He not care? I hear she has been bleeding for twelve years. Now all she has done is touch the hem of Jesus' gown and she is healed. Will my daughter's healing happen as quickly?

But wait! Here come the messengers with news that my daughter has died. They want me to come straight home and not bother with Jesus anymore. My thoughts overwhelm me. Why did Jesus take so long? Why did it seem like He heard my plea and that the answer was on its way? Why did He delay? Jesus overhears our conversation as well as the one going on in my mind and says to me, "Do not be afraid; only believe" (Mark 5:36, NKJV). But I am afraid, and it is difficult to believe that anything more can be done for my daughter, I think, as we head to my home with Peter, James, and John. The crowd is finally behind us.

The mourners have already gone ahead of us and are

causing such a commotion. Jesus admonishes them for wailing so loudly for a child who He says is just asleep. She looks dead to me. The mourners ridicule Him. I want to, as well, but I dare not. I am confused. I am either going to witness a miracle or the greatest disappointment of my life, but in that moment, when it is just Jesus, my wife, some disciples, and I in the room, I begin to feel the peace I can hear in His voice. *"Talitha koum,"* He commands; "Little girl, get up" (Mark 5:41)!

Immediately, our daughter rises and walks around. There is much rejoicing in our home that day; there is also much amazement. What a day it has been! What an emotional roller coaster! As the day ends, I reflect on all that happened- the interruptions on the way and my anxiety at Jesus' delay. Then I realize that Jesus answered my prayer the very first time I prayed: "My little daughter lies at the point of death. Come and lay Your hands on her, that she may be healed, and she will live." Immediately, Jesus went with me. He never left my side.

What I perceived to be delayed prayer had only been an opportunity to build my faith to believe, through all the miracles I had witnessed, that my own miracle was coming.

Before you go: *God's delays might just be opportunities for Him to demonstrate the fullness of His power.*

QUICK STOP: GOD IS A WATCHER

What does this mean? The Psalmist knows this even as he asks the rhetorical question: "I look up to the mountains — does my help come from there? My help comes from the LORD, who made heaven and earth" (Psalm 121:1-2, NLT)! Once he identifies where his help lies, he begins to dig deeper to describe the watchful eyes of God. First, God will not let you stumble because He is a watcher over you; He does not sleep. Secondly, He has not assigned the watchman task to anyone else. As the Psalmist learns, "the LORD Himself watches over you!" He will protect you and keep you from harm. He will not allow the elements to harm you. Finally, the LORD will watch over your life and keep you from harm as a result. He will keep watch over you, today and forever more.

REST STOP 17: A PRAYER OF THANKSGIVING
(PSALM 40:4-5)

"How precious also are Your thoughts to me, O God! How vast is the sum of them" (Psalm 139:17, NASB)! How can I begin to count the thoughts that you think towards me? How can I capture them in the order You think them? No wonder the Psalmist declared, "many, O Lord my God, are your wonderful works which you have done; And your thoughts toward us cannot be recounted to you in order; If I would declare and speak of them, they are more than can be numbered" (Psalm 40:5, NKJV).

You promised to never leave me nor forsake me (Hebrews 13:5). When I wake up in the morning, you are there. When I lay down my head at night, you are there. You stoop down and incline your ears towards me. You hear my laughter; you hear my cries and attend to them. Where can I go to hide from your love? Or from the thoughts you think towards me—the thoughts which you say are of good not evil, to prosper me and not to harm me, to give me a future (Jeremiah 29:11)?

The Psalmist continues, "If I rise on the wings of the dawn, if I settle on the far side of the sea, even there your hand will guide me, your right hand will hold me fast" (Psalm 139:9-10, NIV). Daily my heart beats in rhythm and my lungs take countless breaths. The same heart follows hard after You and the same lungs sing Your praise to the highest heavens. I cannot count the many thoughts You think towards me, but it is enough that Your presence goes with me all my days. You have loved me with an everlasting love and have drawn me with unfailing kindness, and that is more than enough for me (Jeremiah 31:3).

Before you go: *God is always thinking of you. Let that sink in for a moment.*

REST STOP 18: WHEN THE BOTTOM FALLS OUT FROM UNDER YOU
(2 KINGS 19:1-7)

Can you recall a time you received some unexpected and devastating news? You know the type that bursts into your regular routine, determined to knock you off your feet; the type of news that intrudes into your quiet existence with a rude bang? Have you ever felt that you were doing all the right things; that all the balls were in the air, and you were doing well keeping them going, then you dropped one? I have. Where do you go, and to whom do you turn when you experience a seismic shift in the ground you had trusted to hold you up?

Like me, Hezekiah King of Judah, an Old Testament hero of mine, also knew intrusions well. He was a breath of fresh air in a line of kings who had repeatedly failed to honor the Lord their God, worshipping, instead, the gods of the nations around them. The Bible describes him as doing what was pleasing in God's sight and there was no one like him among the kings of Judah, either before or after his time (2 Kings 18:3-5).

Hezekiah had heard about the plight of the people of Samaria at the hands of the Assyrian king and their exile to Assyria. One day he learned that this same King was trying to discredit his leadership and mock his confidence in the God whom he served and trusted. It was not an ordinary day. Hezekiah's army was no match to his Assyrian counterpart's. He could not even rely on his usual ally, the Egyptian army. He assessed the situation before him and knew right away that this war was not going to be won with mere physical might, so he turned to the prophet of God, Isaiah, who assured him of God's promised victory.

With the confidence that God was going to fight on his

behalf, Hezekiah was not moved when the king of Assyria formally served him a letter of declaration of war. Hezekiah marched up to the Lord's Temple, spread the letter out before God and simply prayed for deliverance. God heard his prayer, intervened in the war, and defeated the Assyrians. Hezekiah had a history with God, but it did not mean that he was immune from trouble. It meant that because he had a solid relationship with God, he knew to whom he could turn when the difficult times came.

Difficult times will come and when they do, Hezekiah's story teaches us not to rely on our own human strength and understanding. We have direct access to God and simply need to turn to Him, present our case to the one who always fights on our behalf and expect victory *every time*.

Before you go: *Jesus warned about trials in life, but He promised victory through faith in His finished work on Calvary. This is all the assurance we need when troubled times come.*

REST STOP 19: A VACUUM CLEANER AND A LESSON IN POTENTIAL
(MATTHEW 25:14-30)

About ten years ago, we moved into a new home with a central vacuum system that did not work, so we just kept using our old and faithful Kirby. We did not like lugging it around from room to room and up and down the stairs, but we thought we had no choice. Replacing the Kirby bags when they were full was frustrating; so was the trip across town, to the one shop that we knew still stocked them.

One day, I decided to take another look at our central vacuum system. I went to the basement to inspect the sticker on the receptacle. I was looking for information on the company that serviced it for the previous owners. I found a number and called the company, and they came over and serviced it. All it needed was a new hose. Nowadays, the hose plugged into the wall is the only piece that we move from room to room, and I occasionally wonder why we waited so long to fully maximize the vacuum system's potential.

In many ways, we treat our talents and gifts the way we did our vacuum system. Just as we did not fully realize the potential of what we had sitting in our closet for all those years, we can also operate below our full God-given potential. I am reminded of the parable of the man who was about to embark on a journey. He called his three servants, and gave them five talents, two talents and one talent respectively, "dividing it in proportion to their abilities" (Matthew 25:15, NLT). Though the men were not equally talented, their employer expected them all to steward what they had received very well. Upon his return, the employer discovered that the man with the five talents had doubled his talents. So had the man with two. The man with one talent acted out of fear and ignorance and did nothing with his. He made wrong assumptions about his master's business practices, causing him to miss his full potential.

God has given us all talents as well, dividing them in proportion to our abilities. His expectation is not that we should earn equal returns on our investments. All he requires is that we steward what he has given us to the best of our ability and put it to good use so that, one day, He can say "Well done, good and faithful servant. You have been faithful and trustworthy over a little, I will put you in charge of many things; share in the joy of your master" (Matthew 25:23, AMP).

Now, go and be fruitful and multiply the talents you have been given. It is never too late to begin.

Before you go: *We have all been given a measure of abilities. Ask the Holy Spirit to reveal any undeveloped talents you might have, and when He does, don't spend time on regrets.*

REST STOP 20: CAUTION! CONSTRUCTION SITE
(1 CORINTHIANS 3:1-11)

I work on a college campus, and we have construction going on all the time. What is a college campus without ongoing construction? Each time I take a different route to my office or drive past a new area, I notice that a new building has gone up seemingly overnight. I drove by one of those buildings one day and started to reflect on the building process. I reflected on the concept of building brick by brick, and the importance of laying a solid foundation. I wondered what foundation I am laying as I live my life. Am I building brick by brick? What are the bricks with which I am building?

I thought of my mother and the legacy of faith in Jesus Christ that she is leaving behind in her children and grandchildren. This is the foundation she has laid, and on which she has been building, brick by brick. As Paul says, "for no man can lay a foundation other than the one which is laid, which is Jesus Christ" (1 Corinthians 3:11, NASB). Through my mother's surrender to Jesus Christ, my siblings and I came to faith in Christ and our future generations will be able to relate to the Apostle Paul's words to Timothy: "I remember your genuine faith, for you share the faith that first filled your grandmother Lois and your mother, Eunice. And I know that same faith continues strong in you (2 Timothy 1:5, NLT).

One brick my mother has laid is forgiveness. From childhood, I recall hearing about her choice to forgive the people who had murdered her brother, even though the act left her an only child. As an adult, I have watched her continue to choose forgiveness. She reminded me recently that she can forgive only with the help of Jesus Christ. My mother has also laid the brick of peace. She is a peacemaker and a peacekeeper even when I do not understand it or think it makes sense. She turns the other cheek and gives generously to others.

As I ponder what legacies I am leaving behind for posterity, I realize that I have been an apprentice to a master builder. Brick by brick, because of God's grace to her, my mother has laid the foundation like an expert builder that we, her children, are building on. But we must be very careful. If we build on this foundation using temporal things like gold, silver, costly stones, wood, or straw, our "work will be shown for what it is, because the Day will bring it to light. It will be revealed with fire, and the fire will test the quality of our work (1 Corinthians 3:13, NIV).

The Bible commands us to be careful how we walk, not as unwise men but as wise, making the most of our time, because the days are evil (Ephesians 5:15-16). I do not want to waste my days building on temporal things that will rust or decay, but on things that will have longer lasting impact (2 Corinthians 4:18).

I am grateful for my mother's Godly example and the blueprint that guides me as I build.

Before you go: *We all are master builders, but we must ensure that we are building with bricks that have eternal value.*

QUICK STOP: THE GOD WHO TRANSCENDS SPACE AND TIME

God is not bound by space and time. He responds to prayers prayed from one end of the earth to another. The Syro-Phoenician woman believed this when she approached Jesus and asked Him to deliver her daughter from the unclean spirits which tormented her (Mark 7:2). Although her daughter was at home, she believed that distance would not interfere with her daughter's healing. The centurion also believed the same for his sick servant and asked Jesus to just speak the word so that his servant, who was at home, would be healed, and he was (Matthew 8:8). Whatever you are believing God for today, remember that He is not bound by space and time. The subjects of your prayers may be in distant lands, but the long arm of the Lord extends quite far beyond our imagination.

REST STOP 21: JOY IN THE MORNING
(PSALM 30:4-5)

Yesterday was gloomy and the skies overcast, but the sun is shining brightly this morning. It is not yet spring, but it feels like it, and there is a spring in my steps. The winter months have been too long, and I have missed the warmth of the sun, so today is a very welcome break.

Sometimes we walk through long months or years of winter in our private lives. It may seem like the sun has hidden itself permanently behind the clouds, our feet dragging, and our shoulders slumped. We search for a ray of sunshine to assure us that we are not traveling through an unending night. Then we wake up one morning and the sun is out. She does not announce herself nor give even one clue the day before that the night is ending.

The Psalmist knew this very well when he declared that "weeping may endure for a night, but joy comes in the morning" (Psalm 30:5, NKJV). He was talking about the inevitable: that *trouble don't last always*," according to the old Negro Spiritual. Elsewhere, the Psalmist proclaimed, "those who sow with tears will reap with songs of joy. Those who go out weeping, carrying seed to sow will return with songs of joy, carrying sheaves with them" (Psalm 126:5-6, NIV). He sounds to me like someone who had learned to look for the proverbial silver lining in the sky.

I recently read again about Moses' attempts to get Pharaoh to set the Israelites free from centuries of slavery. "Now the time that the sons of Israel lived in Egypt was four hundred and thirty years" (Exodus 12:40, NASB). That was a long, dark night for the Israelites, but what stood out to me was the fulfillment of the promise God had made to Abraham centuries earlier about this moment of Israel's deliverance. I read, "At the end of four hundred and thirty years, *to the very day*, all the hosts of the LORD went out from the land of Egypt" (Exodus 12:41, NASB). Their deliverance happened not a day early or a day later than when God had promised. How the sun must have shone the day they began their journey of liberty!

As you read this, you may be going through what feels like a long night. It could be a long, dark night of the soul or a long, drawn-out expectancy of something you have been waiting for. Be encouraged and know this: every promise, word of knowledge, revelation, prophecy, that God has spoken to you or over you will happen because he cannot lie. As Habakkuk reminds us: "the vision is yet for an appointed time; but at the end it will speak, and it will not lie. Though it tarries, wait for it; because it will surely come, it will not tarry." (2:3, NKJV).

Today may well be *"the very day!"*

Before you go: *Your life's journey will take you through mountains and valleys, night times and day times, and cloudy days and sunny days. Embrace them all like you would the seasons of the year.*

REST STOP 22: THE WIND BENEATH YOU
(ACTS 2:1-4)

Jesus had risen from the dead and appeared to His disciples to assure them that He was alive, to comfort them in their grief and to give them further instructions on how to occupy until He comes again. He commanded them to wait in Jerusalem for the gift of the Holy Spirit which He had promised them earlier. He was going away, and they needed the Holy Spirit to empower them for the work ahead. In addition to being Jesus' witnesses to the very ends of the earth, the disciples were going to do greater works, in scope, than He had done.

On the day of Pentecost, as promised, the Holy Spirit rushed in like a powerful wind while they were gathered in the upper room and, emboldened by this experience, Peter preached his first message and 3000 people were added to the church in one day.

The promises Jesus made are still for His disciples today. We need the power of the Holy Spirit now more than ever. When we are burdened and weighed down by life's difficulties, it is the Holy Spirit who comes in to help us, sometimes like a might rushing wind, and other times like a gentle breeze. Suddenly, there is a new song on our lips, our eyes shift upwards, our perspective changes, our leaden feet move more swiftly, and we are emboldened to believe for the impossible.

Sometimes, I imagine that the Holy Spirit is in us, like a tailwind, which can propel a plane to fly faster and arrive at its destination in a shorter time. Pilots use this extra help to their advantage, and we, too, can choose to rely on the promised Holy Spirit to come alongside to propel us when we need a second wind.

Before you go*: There is nothing God has asked of you that you can do without the power of the Holy Spirit.*

REST STOP 23: SETTING UP SIGNPOSTS
(JEREMIAH 31:21)

Our lives are like well-traveled roads. There are skid marks, potholes and wrecks that mark various points along the journey. There are also rest stops of joy, blessings and victory. Like ours, the Israelites' journey to the Promised land of Canaan was filled with many significant moments – grumblings, murmurings and complaints, and instances of God's patience, faithfulness and love. In the land of Canaan, they were supposed to be guided by God's laws. They disobeyed these laws and, as a result, God allowed them to be carried into captivity by the Babylonians.

God did not forget about His people in exile. Jeremiah was one of the prophets He sent to assure them that brighter days were ahead. He promised to return them to their land. But God wanted them to remember the way they had traveled. He instructed them, "Set up road signs; put up guideposts. Mark well the path by which you came" (Jeremiah 31:21, NLT).

There is merit to remembering the roads we have traveled because they remind us of God's faithfulness. God may be instructing you today to never forget the way He has led you, and when you have come through, to be grateful. Remember that you have not traveled in your own strength. It is because of the Lord's mercies that we are not consumed because His compassions fail not (Lamentations 3:22).

Just as He commanded the Israelites through Jeremiah, we should set up road signs and guideposts to remind us of His provisions along the way. They will also serve as memorials for those coming behind us. When the time comes, and your children and children's children ask, "What do these mean?" and "What happened here?" you will be able to say of every point, signpost, experience, and God-encounter, that each one was an

Ebenezer (a stone of help) to remind you of God's help every step of the way (1 Samuel 7:12).

Before you go*: "Always be prepared to give an answer to everyone who asks you to give the reason for the hope that you have" (1 Peter 3:15, NIV).*

QUICK STOP: GOD'S FIRST RESPONDERS

What do first responders do? They are the first to run headlong into danger while others are running in the opposite direction. They put their lives on the line in order to minister to others. God has His own first responders, too! In Hebrews 1:14, angels are described as ministering spirits, servants, sent to serve us who will inherit salvation. We are also assured in Psalm 91:11 that God will command His angels concerning us to guard us in all our ways. God's angels have been empowered by Him to hear His commands and fulfil them (Psalm 103:20). Let us remember, then, that even before our earthly first responders arrive on the scene of our troubles, God's first responders have already beaten them to the scene.

REST STOP 24: KEEP THIS FIRMLY IN MIND
(DEUTERONOMY 4:39-40)

I woke up this morning from a dream that troubled my spirit. I prayed about it and committed it to God; yet, all day, I could not shake off the downcast feeling in my spirit. I went about the day's business with the dream weighing on my mind. My early morning dreams are usually prophetic, and I did not like this one. I did not want to engage in spiritual warfare.

I knew from experience that I needed to spend some time in the Word to shift my perspective. Speaking of God's Word, the Psalmist declared, "The entrance of Your word gives light; It gives understanding to the simple" (Psalm 119:130, NKJV), and "Your word is a lamp to my feet and a light to my path" (Psalm 119:105, NKJV). Although I was aware of these scriptures, I had allowed myself to be distracted by busy work which did not bring the peace I desired. Finally, I stopped, went into my closet and settled down to read from Deuteronomy 4. I wondered why Moses was recapping Israel's past experiences with God. As I read, I soon learned why.

Although Moses knew he would not enter the Promised land with the rest of his people, he needed to remind them of God's powerful acts up until that moment as they traveled through the wilderness. He described their deliverance from captivity in Egypt with miraculous signs, wonders and God's powerful arm. He did not want the Israelites to forget all that God had done for them after they entered the Promised land. Moses told them, "so, remember this and keep it *firmly* in mind: The LORD is God both in heaven and on earth, and there is no other" (Deuteronomy 4:39, NLT).

As I recited this burden-lifting, yoke-destroying revealed Word of God, I could feel the burden I had carried all day begin to quickly lift. I declared to myself, "What is this thing that I have not been able to shake off all day compared to my God, the Creator and ruler of the heavens and the earth? He is God, not only in heaven, but also on earth. There is no god besides Him and there is no earthly burden that is not subject to Him."

In that moment, I thanked God for His Word which is alive and powerful, and I thanked Him for the reminder that the Spirit alone gives eternal life. Human effort accomplishes nothing. And the very words God has spoken to me are spirit and life (Hebrews 4:12; John 6:63). With the joy and peace that now overwhelmed me, I sought out my young adult children to share how my burden had been lifted, and how God had communicated with my spirit through His Word.

Before you go: *Don't wait until you are done with your daily chores to sit at God's feet and be strengthened by His life-giving Word.*

REST STOP 25: JUST ONE ENCOUNTER WITH GOD
(LUKE 19:1-10)

When Zacchaeus heard that Jesus was making His way through town, the notoriously rich chief tax collector wanted to see Him. As Jesus headed towards Jerusalem, He healed the sick, taught the people and challenged the religious leaders. Zacchaeus was curious to see this Jesus, about whom he had heard so much. The Bible says he found a sycamore fig tree and climbed it to get a better vantage point.

Zacchaeus was a despised tax-collector who had accumulated his wealth from overtaxing the citizens. People like him had been described as "scum" in Matthew's Gospel (Matthew 9:11, NLT). Jesus had apparently heard about Zacchaeus because he looked up, called him by name, and invited Himself to dinner—all to the amazement of the religious folk. Zacchaeus responded quickly and with excitement.

We need to note here that Jesus was on a mission; he was headed to Jerusalem where he was going to be crucified, but he had to make this important stop. This was not a chance meeting for Jesus. He knew that Zacchaeus needed an encounter with Him. He was not put off by Zacchaeus' sins; instead, Jesus was drawn to him. And once he stood before Jesus, Zacchaeus was immediately convicted of his sins and promised to make restitution to all those he had cheated.

Jesus did not preach a word about Zacchaeus' sins to him. Nor did He utter one word of condemnation. Zacchaeus repented because *Salvation* had come to his home that day. Jesus commended him, saying, "for this man has shown himself to be a true son of Abraham. For the Son of Man came to seek and save those who are lost" (Luke 19:9-10, NLT). Zacchaeus was lost but probably did not know how lost he was. Jesus (whose name means Salvation) visited him. Salvation came to Zacchaeus, drawn by his desire to make a connection to the Savior. It is remarkable that in Luke's Gospel, this was the last personal encounter that Jesus had with an individual before His arrest. Jesus had to stop for Zacchaeus.

Why did Jesus call Zacchaeus a true son of Abraham? Abraham is the Father of faith. He believed God when there was no tangible evidence of God's promises that his descendants would be as numerous as the stars; therefore, all who come after Abraham, who are moved by their faith in God and not their circumstances, are called the children of Abraham. It was by faith that Zacchaeus climbed the sycamore tree to see Jesus. It was by faith that, when Jesus called out to him, he immediately responded. Zacchaeus did not allow his sins or reputation to hinder his connection with Jesus.

Today, no matter where you are or what is going on with you, remember that just one encounter with God is all you need: just one moment in His presence, just one word of revelation. And when he calls you, when you feel his Spirit tugging at your heart, answer immediately, with excitement as Zacchaeus did. You never know what miracles lie at the end of your "Yes." As God has promised, when we seek Him with all our hearts, we will find Him (Jeremiah 29:13).

Before you go: *Jesus responds to the longing we have for Him in our hearts. When we sincerely seek Him, He responds and invites Himself into our hearts.*

QUICK STOP: FEAR IS A LIAR

A popular song, *Fear is a Liar,* by Jason Ingram, Zach Williams, and Jonathan Lindley Smith reminds us that fear is a real, tangible thing. It comes to cloud your mind and rob you of joy. Everything fear speaks is contrary to God's Word. It may speak to the reality of your current circumstances, but it doesn't have the final say. God's Word does. So when fear says that your circumstances will never change, remember that God's Word says that "weeping may endure for a night, but joy comes in the morning" (Psalm 30:5, NKJV) If fear tells you that God has forgotten you, remind it that God's Word says "Can a woman forget her nursing child, and have no compassion on the son of her womb? Even these may forget, but I will not forget you" (Isaiah 49:15, NASB). God's Word is truth, and it assures us that "God has not given us a spirit of fear, but a spirit of love, of power and of a sound mind" (2 Timothy 1:7, NKJV). Fear is a spirit, so when it comes, speak to it and command it to leave. Feed on the truth of God's Word, so that you can counter fear's attacks.

REST STOP 26: GOD IS ALWAYS AT WORK
(JOHN 5:1-17)

Waymaker, a popular song by Gospel singer Osinachi Joseph, popularly known as Sinach, has literally taken the whole world by storm. It has crossed cultural, racial and national boundaries and has been translated into many languages. It is a song that resonates with many people because of the encouragement it brings, the reassurance that when things look like they are staying the same, when our circumstances seem like they will not be changing any time soon, our God is still at work. The wide appeal of this song reminds me of the universal human need for patience and hope while we wait for God's promises to be fulfilled.

Over 2000 years ago, Jesus expressed a similar truth to the Jewish leaders who were so diligent about keeping the Sabbath laws that they neglected to make room for God's grace to change lives. Jesus had just healed the disabled man who had been lying by the pool of Bethesda for thirty-eight years. It was a Sabbath day, a day of rest when adherents of the law are not supposed to engage in manual labor. The religious people were offended that the man broke the law by picking up and folding his mat as Jesus had instructed; although, I think they were more offended with Jesus for healing the man on a Sabbath. Jesus had to remind them that "the Sabbath was made to meet the needs of people, and not people to meet the requirements of the Sabbath" (Mark 2: 27-28, NLT).

In response to their harassing remarks about working on the sabbath, Jesus announced, "My Father is always working, and so am I" (John 5:17, NLT). He continued, "I tell you the truth, the Son can do nothing by Himself. He does only what He sees His Father doing. Whatever the Father does, the Son also does.

For the Father loves the Son and shows Him everything He is doing" (John 5:19-20, NLT).

Jesus was teaching them that He did not come to break the law, but to be obedient to the assignments He received from His Father. It is reassuring to be reminded that God and Jesus are always at work. In fact, Jesus sits at God's right hand praying for us all the time, and if His Father shows Him everything He is doing, then we have no better prayer partner than Jesus.

Are you impatient when you don't see visible evidence that God is at work in your life? You are not alone! We all don't do well with not knowing the behind–the–scenes quiet workings of God. We forget that He is the Master weaver, always working and casting the many threads of our lives at the loom. Even when the patterns don't make sense, we should just trust that when he is done, we will behold a series of beautiful master pieces along our life's journey. Selah!

Before you go: *Remember that the potter at the wheel has one goal: to create a masterpiece. He works the imperfections in the clay into a piece that is perfect in his eyes.*

REST STOP 27: GOD IS OUR ANCHOR
(DEUTERONOMY 10:20; 11:22)

As I write this, the nation is literally burning. Another black man has died after he was brutally assaulted by police officers for using a counterfeit $20 bill. This time around, more people across the racial spectrum have been touched in a deeper way and are protesting. Even though this tragedy is not unusual, the call for racial injustice has never been louder. For a moment it seems that we have forgotten that the COVID-19 virus is still raging. The people are raging, the fires are raging, and even the earth is raging with tornados, earthquakes and volcanic eruptions.

As the world rages, everything feels uncertain and the things and places we thought we could rely on are failing us. What are we to do when everything around is unstable? When the things we previously looked to for stability are themselves shaken, where do we turn for some stability? It is easy to slip into despair and accept hopelessness as the current norm. But we have an anchor in God. Moses tried to convey this to the Israelites on the journey to the land God had promised to their ancestors. He commanded them to fear the Lord, worship Him and cling to Him (Deuteronomy 10:20). In Deuteronomy 11:22, he reminded them to obey God's commands, walk in His ways and hold tightly to Him.

They were heading towards the unknown, but Moses was reminding them of the one thing that was known—the God who was leading them through the wilderness and who had already gone before them into the Promised land. What Moses was promising them may have seemed daunting: that God would drive out all the inhabitants of the land toward which He was leading them; that they would possess every piece of land they stepped foot on; and that they would be feared by the inhabitants of the land.

Moses knew that they would not be able to face the future without walking closely with and holding on to God. He wanted them to understand that the God who had led them out of Egypt and through the wilderness would never leave their side. All He required of them was obedience, to commit themselves wholeheartedly to His commands.

Just as He did many thousands of years ago with the Israelites, God is giving us the same choices today. In these uncertain times, we can cling to the God who has promised to always be with us. We can cling to the blessings that come from obeying His Word or we can cling to the curses that come from rejecting God's Word. I choose to cling to the former, for experience has taught me that it is in holding tightly to Him that I find the only place that cannot be shaken.

Before you go: *When the ground under you is unstable, find refuge in God and His Word; both will never fail you.*

QUICK STOP: FIX YOUR EYES ON JESUS

I suffer from motion sickness, but I have learned the trick to surviving boat rides: find an object and fix your eyes on it. When I do that, I am okay and can finish the ride regardless of the turbulence in the waters. I am reminded of Peter's near drowning incidence when he failed to maintain his gaze on Jesus. One night, while the disciples were alone in a boat, Jesus came walking toward them on the water. When Peter saw Him, he asked to join the Master, and at Jesus' invitation, Peter went walking on the water towards Jesus. As long as Peter kept his gaze on Jesus, he had nothing to fear. When he took his eyes off Jesus, and focused on the turbulent waters, he lost his footing and started to sink. Life guarantees turbulent times, but we can remain sure-footed when we find that fixed, immoveable focal point, Jesus, and keep our eyes steadfastly on Him.

REST STOP 28: GOD'S MASTER PLAN–A PARADOX?
(ACTS 9: 1-5)

God, speaking through the prophet Isaiah, thousands of years before the birth of the Church, promised to destroy the wisdom of the wise, the intelligence of the intelligent and make human wisdom look foolish (Isaiah 29:14). In the New Testament, Paul's message to the Church at Corinth began with what may seem to its listeners to be a paradox: God chooses the foolish things of the world to confound those who think they are wise; the weak things to shame those who think they are powerful; and those whom the world despises, he uses to confuse and bring to nothing those who think they are important. And God does all this so that no one can boast of themselves before him (1 Corinthians 1:27-29).

I am very thankful for this God who chooses whom He wills and when He wills to further His work. The story of Saul, who later became Paul and wrote a significant portion of the New Testament, is a perfect illustration. The Church was still very new in the Book of Acts and the world at the time was a dangerous place for believers. But even though Jesus Christ had been killed, His disciples had come out of hiding and were boldly proclaiming the Good News of the kingdom. One of them, a young man named Stephen, found himself facing imminent death because of his faith. He was dragged out of the city to be stoned.

The Bible takes the time to tell us that while Stephen was being stoned, his accusers laid their coats at the feet of another young man named Saul. This is our first introduction to Saul who, even though he did not cast a stone at Stephen, gave his silent approval of his murder and went on to become a well-known persecutor of the early church.

Stephen's death marked the beginning of great persecution of the early Church and created the atmosphere for widespread violence against the early believers. Saul went everywhere, from house to house, dragging out men and women and throwing them in prison (Acts 8:3). But God had His own plans. He always does, even in the face of the world's plans. The persecution of the Church did not hinder its growth; instead, the believers who scattered spread the Good News of the Gospel wherever they went. As the Church grew, opportunities for persecution grew, and Saul eagerly found his way to Damascus to arrest followers of Jesus there.

We do not read anywhere, between his role in Stephen's death and his journey to Damascus, that Saul had second thoughts about his violence towards Jesus' followers; instead, it appeared that his zeal only grew stronger. It was in this depraved state of mind that Jesus accosted him, stopping him in his destructive tracks. Jesus had a divine assignment for Saul. He wanted him to be His chosen instrument to take the message of the Gospel to both Jews and non-Jews, kings and peasants.

It was not to any of the apostles that Jesus turned to carry out His master plan. He turned to a man who had done unspeakable things to the Church, a man whose zeal against the Church now turned towards church growth. Saul immediately began preaching about Jesus and testifying that He was the Son of God, to the amazement of all who knew of his past. Jesus had indeed chosen a foolish vessel and confounded those who were wise in their own eyes.

Throughout the New Testament we read of Jesus' many encounters with the rejected, the forgotten, the people who had been discarded by society. Today, He still seeks to demonstrate His grace and mercy in and through the most unlikely of persons and situations. We should learn from Saul's conversion that God has a master plan for each one of us and it usually never makes sense to us. We cannot write off any person or situation as irredeemable because God, alone, has the final say. And who knows if one of these persons or situations will be the ones to turn our world, today, upside down (Acts 17:6)

Before you go*: There is no person or situation that is too far gone to be redeemed by God.*

REST STOP 29: OUT OF ONE, MANY
(GENESIS 17:1-8)

The traditional motto of the United States, *E pluribus unum* (out of many, one) speaks to the strength that is found in the diversity of its population. It is indeed a strength that has been demonstrated over and over; a rare but beautiful thing that takes effort to continue to maintain. God chose to do something even more extraordinary and miraculous when He decided that out of one man, He would start a family for His own glory.

Thousands of years ago, a man named Abram (who God later renamed Abraham) had a conversation with God. Abram was childless and longed for an heir. God took him outside at night, told him to look up at the stars and promised that He would make Abram's descendants as countless as those stars in the sky. Abram literally took God at his Word and God took note and "counted him as righteous because of his faith" (Genesis 15:6, NLT). After ten years of waiting, it seemed like God's promise was not going to come to pass after all, so Abram's wife, Sarai, persuaded him to take her maidservant, Hagar, as his wife. Hagar gave birth to a son, Ishmael, but he was not the heir of promise. God's masterplan had not changed.

Thirteen years after the birth of Ishmael, God appeared again to Abram and repeated the covenant He had made with him many years before. Although Abram had faltered, God's promise still stood sure. God renewed His promise to Abram that he would be the father of many nations and changed his name to Abraham to reflect his new status. God promised Abraham, "I will confirm my covenant with you and your descendants after you, from generation to generation. This is the everlasting covenant: I will always be your God and the God of your descendants after you" (Genesis 17:7, NLT).

It is remarkable that twenty-five years passed before God blessed Abraham and Sarai with the promised son, Isaac, who became the Father of the nation of Israel. But without a reference point, Abraham could not have imagined what we have the privilege of knowing today: that we who believe God, and by faith receive Jesus Christ as Lord and Savior, are included in the descendants about which God spoke. We, as believers, are a part of the descendants who continue to grow daily as people everywhere come to Christ by faith, are made right with God and are grafted into the covenant God made with Abraham.

Thousands of years later, in a letter to the Roman believers, Paul referred to that covenant between Abraham and God. Paul, who was God's chosen instrument to take the Good News of the Gospel to everyone, Jew and Greek alike, explained how "because of Abraham's faith, God counted him as righteous. And when God counted him as righteous, it wasn't just for Abraham's benefit. It was recorded for our benefit, too, assuring us that God will also count us as righteous if we believe in him, the one who raised Jesus our Lord from the dead" (Romans 4:23-24, NLT).

Today we are participants in, and recipients of, the deep riches of God's covenant with Abraham, established thousands of years ago when God spoke of a divine multiplication plan that transcended human understanding—of how generations to come would believe Him by faith and be adopted into Abraham's genealogy, and how the literal and spiritual nations which came from him would continue to grow exponentially, unstoppable, through the ages.

E pluribus unum (out of many, one) is man's idea but OUT OF ONE, MANY is a miracle that continues to resound through the ages, upheld by the Word of promise God made to one man.

Before you go: *God is a multiplier. Through our faith in Jesus Christ, we have been engrafted into God's spiritual family and become a part of the countless descendants God promised Abraham.*

QUICK STOP: GOD IS A HASTENER

God spoke to His children about their future while they were still in exile in Babylon. He promised to put His favor on them and return them from exile with joy, bearing the wealth of many lands. Their return would be spectacular and all nations who witnessed their exile and gloated over it, would come and bow before them. Regarding the timing of His visitation, God promised: "At the right time, I, the LORD, will make it happen" (Isaiah 60:22, NLT). Another translation says, "I, the Lord, will hasten it in its time" (NASB). The same God promised elsewhere, "I will hasten my word to perform it" (Jeremiah 1:12, KJV). At just the right time, God stirred the heart of King Cyrus of Persia to proclaim freedom to God's people, thereby hastening their return to Jerusalem. And as God promised, they returned with all that had been stolen from them, including the wealth of the Babylonians. God is the Creator of time; therefore, when Peter says that "A day is like a thousand years to the Lord, and a thousand years is like a day" (2 Peter 3:8, NLT), we must understand that whatever our circumstances, they could very well change in an instant if we will just believe His promises. If we trust Him, we know that He will do the right thing at the right time, but we should leave the when and how to Him.

REST STOP 30: THE LORD IS MARCHING AHEAD OF YOU
(JUDGES 4:1-23)

I am overwhelmed this morning as I am reminded that the moments of our lives are not randomly organized–not even the ones which seem small and insignificant. I am reading from the Book of Judges about people who lived thousands of years ago. Writing today's date as I take notes, I am struck by the familiarity of the date. Five years ago, on this day, my father lay dying in the hospital after I had spent many long and difficult days sleeping by his side and praying for his healing. As I fought for my fathers' life, I could not have imagined that anything else would ever consume my thoughts, or that I would ever desperately need God again.

But in the five years since then, so many other things have happened that I could not have imagined back then; yet, in all of them, God has delivered me. In the many moments of our lives, especially when we are amid trials, it is difficult to see or imagine the way out, but we have a God who marches ahead of us. He knows there is a way out because He has made provision for our escape.

The book of Judges tells the story of Deborah, who ruled Israel as a judge when God had just turned Israel over to their enemy, King Jabin of Hazor. She had to come up with a strategy to defeat King Jabin's ruthless commander, Sisera. Amid the narrative, it seems like some random piece of information is dropped into the mix. There was an Israelite named Heber, who had moved and pitched his tent away from the other members of his tribe. This was unusual because, at that time, people tended to live alongside members of their tribe. In addition to what we later learn was a strategic relocation, was the friendship between Heber and King Jabin. These two factors positioned Heber's wife, Jael, to be used to kill Sisera who escaped from the war after he abandoned his army and took refuge in Heber's tent, believing he was safe in Jael's hands.

I doubt that when Heber moved away from the rest of his tribe or when the friendship was formed between his family and King Jabin, that he knew that these two factors would play a role in defeating Sisera and, ultimately, King Jabin. But God knew. Deborah was confident about Israel's victory, hence her declaration to Barak, the leader of Israel's army, "Get ready! This is the day the LORD will give you victory over Sisera, for the LORD is marching ahead of you" (Judges 4:14, NLT).

Five years ago, God was marching ahead of me. He knew what lay ahead and had already made provision for His grace which would be more than enough for each season. What will the next five years bring? I do not have any idea, but I am confident that just as He did through Heber's relocation and friendship with King Jabin, He will take all the seemingly random moments and events of the moment and cause them to work out into some good things. I am encouraged that I don't journey alone. I have a guide and a way maker. All I must do is get ready and follow.

Before you go: *God will take the seemingly random moments of your life and work them into unimaginable good. Just trust Him.*

FINAL WORD: DISCONNECTED FROM THE BASE

The wireless phone handsets in our home had been acting up for months. We finally decided to replace them. The handsets have a home base which serves as a control center for the entire system. I noticed that as soon as we disconnected the home base from the power source, all the other handsets lost their connection as well and their screens read, "disconnected from the base." I immediately had an "Aha" moment because I saw a spiritual connection—the handsets drew their power from the home base which drew its power from the home's power source. The entire system needed to be connected to a power source to function properly.

After His resurrection, Jesus appeared to His disciples and promised: "I will send the Holy Spirit, just as my Father promised. But stay here in the city until the Holy Spirit comes and fills you with power from heaven" (Luke 24:49, NLT). In Luke's epistle, these were Jesus' last words to His disciples. Jesus was going back to His Father and was assuring His disciples that power would be made available to them to continue the work of spreading the Gospel. Fifty days after the promise, on the day of Pentecost, the disciples received the promised Holy Spirit and were radically transformed from the fearful disciples they had become after Jesus' crucifixion, into bold and courageous carriers of the Gospel — an assignment they would not have been able to accomplish in their own strength.

In our daily living, it is easy for us to slip into self-suffici-ent mode and operate in our own mental, emotional, and physical strength. It is no wonder we soon become weary and struggle to complete even the simplest tasks. Just like our phone system's disconnected warning, I also get an alert when I am unplugged from the Holy Spirit. I get a warning when I rely on my strength to produce "love, joy, peace, patience, kindness, goodness, faithfulness, gentleness, and self-control" and a reminder to return to my power source to be recharged (Galatians 5:22-23, NLT).

I discovered not too long ago that I could print documents from my smart phone and that all I need to do is discover the printers to which my phone is connected wirelessly. I was excited at this discovery and wondered what else is available to me that I am missing. These moments cause me to wonder why I choose to labor in my own strength when Jesus has made all power available to me through the Holy Spirit. When Jesus offered the invitation, "Come to Me, all who are weary and heavy-laden, and I will give you rest" (Matthew 11:28, NASB), He was asking us to exchange our labor for His rest, our tendencies for self-sufficiency for reliance on His power.

The devotionals in this book have been invitations to stop, steal away and spend time in the Word of God. In God's Word is where you will find everything you will ever need on life's journey, "for as you know Him better, He will give you, through His great power, everything you need for living a truly good life: He even shares His own glory and His own goodness with us" (2 Peter 1:3, TLB)! I pray you will continue to practice the spiritual principle of rest even when you are finished with this book.

By His Grace,

Chinwe Okpalaoka

www.ingramcontent.com/pod-product-compliance
Lightning Source LLC
Chambersburg PA
CBHW071504070426
42452CB00041B/2282